D1061552

YOUR GREATEST POWER

by J. MARTIN KOHE

Enlarged Edition

Combined Registry Company

Chicago, Illinois 60640

The Choice Is Yours

An Introduction by W. Clement Stone

→»>-»>-»>«<-«<-«<

POWERS . . . YOU HAVE THEM. BUT YOU MAY NOT choose to use them. For some are so obvious you don't recognize them. Thus you may not *intentionally* choose to use what J. Martin Kohe discovered to be *your greatest power* . . . power you, and every boy and girl, man and woman, possess.

Peace of mind . . . happiness . . . physical, mental and moral health . . . success and wealth . . . have come to those who have read *Your Greatest Power*, authored by J. Martin Kohe, and *deliberately* used the secret which it reveals.

Hundreds of thousands of lives . . . perhaps millions . . . have been changed for the better because of Mr. Kohe. For he was the publisher and distributor of inspirational self-help books. Examples: *Think and Grow Rich* and *Law of Success*. During his lifetime he kept striving for the knowledge that would help him and others become better persons and lead truly successful lives. Because he searched so diligently, he made the discovery which he reveals in his book *Your Greatest Power*.

As President of Combined Insurance Company of America and its subsidiaries, I have been amazed to find how great a motivating influence this little book has had on the lives of our sales representatives and office personnel.

As President of The Chicago Boys Clubs I have used *Your Greatest Power* to awaken the teenager to his power *voluntarily* to control himself and find the true riches of life as well as success in school, sports and the activities in which he wishes to excel.

As an associate of Bill Sands, the author of *My Shadow Ran Fast*, I have seen the power in *Your Greatest Power* inspire prisoners in The 7th Step Foundation program *intentionally* and successfully strive to re-habilitate themselves.

As director of several organizations interested in mental health, I have observed that *Your Greatest Power* has given hope to the emotionally disturbed and the alcoholic.

Your Greatest Power is exciting and easy to read. Its charm is in its simplicity; its strength in its sincerity. But most of all, it inspires and moves you to desirable action. Your life too can be changed for the better when you *voluntarily* choose to use your greatest power.

W. Clement Stone

YOUR GREATEST POWER

Your Greatest Power

Discovering It

->>>->>>->>> <<<-<<<-<<<-

YOU ARE THE POSSESSOR OF A GREAT AND wonderful power. This power, when properly applied, will bring confidence instead of timidity, calmness instead of confusion, poise instead of restlessness, and peace of mind in place of a heartache.

Millions of people are complaining about their lot, disgusted with life . . . and the way things are going, not realizing that there is a power which they possess which will permit them to take a new lease on life. Once you recognize this power and begin to use it, you can change your entire life and make it the way you would like to have it. A life that was filled with sorrow can be a life filled with joy. Failure can be turned into success. Where poverty once gripped an individual's life, it can be changed to prosperity. Timidity can be turned into confidence. A life of disappointment can become

[1]

a life of interesting experiences and pleasant associations. Fear can be changed to freedom.

Too many times, as life goes on, a person may have had a number of reverses, he may have run into a series of difficulties, he may even have had a number of various troubles to contend with. Before long he adopts the attitude that life is difficult, that life is a battle, that the cards are stacked against him . . . so what's the use . . ."you can't win." Then this same individual settles back and is convinced that no matter what you do is "no good." Beaten in his own desire to win in life, he finally turns to his children, hoping that with them it will be different. Sometimes, this is a way out, and sometimes the children fall into the same way of life as the parent. Many times the individual comes to the conclusion that there is only one way out, and he finally comes to the end of life through his own hand . . . suicide.

Yet, all this time, the individual fails to discover this great power that will change his life. He doesn't recognize it . . . he doesn't even know it exists . . . he sees millions of others struggling the way he is and decides that THIS IS LIFE.

Raimundo DeOvies tells a story that, when the great library of Alexandria was burned, one book was saved. But it was not a valuable book; and so a poor man, who could read a little, bought it for a few coppers. It was not very interesting; yet there was a most interesting thing in it! It was a thin strip of vellum on which was written the secret of the "Touchstone."

The touchstone was a small pebble that could turn any common metal into pure gold. The writing explained that it was on the shores of the Black Sea, lying among thousands and thousands of other pebbles which looked exactly like it. But the secret was this. The real stone would feel warm, while ordinary pebbles are cold. So the man sold his few belongings, bought some simple supplies, camped on the seashore, and began testing pebbles. This was his plan.

He knew that if he picked up ordinary pebbles and threw them down again because they were cold, he might pick up the same pebble hundreds of times. So, when he felt one that was cold, he threw it into the sea. He spent a whole day doing this and there were none of them the touchstone. Then he spent a week, a month, a year, three years; but he did not find the touchstone. Yet he went on and on this way. Pick up a pebble. It's cold. Throw it into the sea. And so on and on.

But one morning he picked up a pebble and it was *warm* . . . he threw it into the sea. He had formed the "habit" of throwing them into the sea. He had gotten so into the habit of throwing them into the sea, that when the ONE HE WANTED CAME ALONG . . . HE STILL THREW IT AWAY.

Oh! How many times have we contacted this GREAT POWER and did not recognize it? How many times have we had THIS GREAT POWER right in our hands and we threw it away, because we did not recognize it? How often have we seen it before our very eyes? How many times have we seen THIS GREAT POWER demonstrated right before us? Yet, we did not see it with all its possibilities, with all its wonder-working effects. That is the reason we have devoted this entire treatise to THIS GREAT POWER . . . THE GREATEST POWER THAT MAN POSSESSES!

Conwell, in his book, "Acres of Diamonds," tells about a farmer who was a very happy farmer. His farm was all paid off. He had a very lovely family. Each year he managed to save some money from his plantings. He wasn't short of anything to make his life worthwhile and happy. However, one day a traveler came along and said to the farmer, "If you will find a place where water runs over white sand, there you will find diamonds. Your daughter will be richer than any princess, your son will be richer than any prince, and you will have all the wealth that you could possibly imagine." That night this farmer did not sleep . . . for the first time in many months. He rolled and tossed and turned. Finally when dawn broke he decided he would sell his farm and go out and search for diamonds. This he did. He put his family in with one of the neighbors, took his money and went all over the world searching for diamonds. Finally, when he came down to his last few cents, thoroughly disgusted with himself and what he had done, he committed suicide. In the meantime, the traveler returned to the farm. He walked into the house, looked up on the mantelpiece, and exclaimed, "Did the original owner of the farm return?" The new owner said, "No, he did not." The traveler said, "He must have, why those stones up there on the mantelpiece are diamonds." "Oh! no," exclaimed the new owner of the farm, "that's impossible . . . I found those stones out in the back yard." The traveler again as-

sured the new owner, "Yes, those are diamonds." That is the way the Kimberley
Diamond Mines in Africa were founded.

Certainly, you see the point in the story.
We search all over the world looking for
diamonds and still, there they are right in
our own back yards. We search all through
our lives for THAT POWER which will
make our lives complete, but most people
never find it. Yet, it is right before us. All
we have to do is recognize it and start to use
it. It's here.

Before we tell you what this GREAT
POWER is, we want you to know about another story that took place in Africa. There
was an explorer who went into the wilds of
Africa. He took a number of trinkets along
with him for the natives. Among some of
the things that he took with him were two
full-size mirrors. He placed these two mirrors against two different trees, and then sat
down to talk to some of his men about the
exploration. Then the explorer noticed that
a savage approached the mirror with a
spear in his hand. As he looked into the mirror, he saw his reflection. He began to jab
his opponent in the mirror as though it were
a real savage, going through all the motions
of killing him. Of course, he broke the mirror into bits. In the meantime, the explorer

walked over to the savage and asked him why he smashed the mirror. The native replied, "He go kill me. I kill him first." The explorer explained to the savage that that was not the purpose of the mirror, and then led the savage over to the second mirror. He explained to him. "Look, the mirror is an object whereby you may see if your hair is combed straight, to see if the paint on your face is proper, to see how chesty you are, and see how muscular you are." The savage replied, "Oh! me no know."

So it is with so many millions of people. They go through life fighting it. They expect a battle at every turn and that is the way it turns out. They expect to have enemies, and they certainly do. They expect to have one difficulty after another, and that is exactly the way it happens. "If it isn't one thing, it's another . . . there is always something" . . . and that is the way it has been and will continue to be for millions of people who fail to recognize this GREAT POWER. This GREAT POWER that could completely change the world remains as hidden as the diamonds from the farmer who had them in his own back yard. Millions of people will continue to live plain, ordinary, miserable lives because this GREAT POWER escapes them and they never have been able to catch up with it. YOU CAN'T FIGHT LIFE. You have tried it. Millions have tried it and have failed. Then what is the answer? THE ANSWER IS THAT WE MUST UNDERSTAND LIFE . . . IF WE WISH TO MAKE THE MOST OF IT.

The amazing part about this power is that anyone and everyone can use it. It doesn't require any special training or education. It isn't a power that requires any special aptitudes to make it work successfully. It isn't a power that anyone has any special claims to, nor does it require wealth or prestige to make it work. It is a power that everyone is given at birth, whether he be rich or poor, successful or unsuccessful, whether he be born on the right side of the tracks or not. The sooner we recognize this power, the quicker we get on the main road and stay there. The more of us who will get on the main road and stay there, the more hope will spring in the hearts of others to follow this healthy pattern of life.

Millions of people fail to realize that when they go into a shoe store, they may choose to buy a pair of black shoes or they may choose to buy a pair of brown shoes; that when they go into a clothing store, they choose to buy a light garment or they choose to buy a dark garment; that when they turn on the radio they may choose to tune in one station or they may choose to tune in another station; that when they go into an ice cream parlor, they may choose to buy a chocolate sundae or a pineapple soda; that when they go to the movies, they may choose to go to a neighborhood movie or they may choose to go to a downtown movie. Yes, it is true, if you CHOOSE, when you go on a vacation, to go to the seashore instead of going to the mountains, that YOU MADE THIS CHOICE. When you buy a car YOU CHOOSE to buy a car of one particular make or YOU CHOOSE to buy a car of another manufacturer. In other words, THE GREATEST POWER THAT A PERSON POSSESSES IS

THE POWER TO CHOOSE.

Yes, you have this power, regardless of your religious beliefs. You choose the shoes, the car, the radio program, the picture show, the vacation, the mate. You have this power. There was nothing outside of yourself to force you to make the decision that you did. You did it, because you made this choice. You made this choice because YOU WANTED IT SO. If the choice was bad, then, of course, we want something or someone to blame. So, some people will say, "It was God's Will." But was it? You are probably familiar with the old saying "God helps those that help themselves." Regardless of what we believe regarding God, God does give each and every man and woman the right TO HELP HIMSELF . . . OR IN OTHER WORDS, *THE RIGHT TO CHOOSE.*

Henry Drummond in his book "The Greatest Thing in the World" tells a story of a little boy who was very sick. The boy was going to die. The parents were very much upset about it, and yet, there was nothing the doctors could do. One day an elderly, religious man walked into the house and noticed how depressed everyone was. He asked why they were so downhearted. He was told that their little son was very sick and they expected the little fellow to die. The religious man asked where the boy was and he was told which bedroom to go to. The elderly religious man walked into the bedroom, put his hand on the little fellow's head and said, "My boy, GOD LOVES YOU, don't you know that?" and walked out of the room, then shortly afterward left the home. After he had gone, the little fellow who was sick and was going to die, jumped out of bed, ran all over the house shouting, "God loves me . . . GOD LOVES ME."

He no longer was sick, but a well, strong and healthy boy.

Here is a perfect illustration of what happens when a person CHOOSES to believe that God loves him. No doubt, the little fellow had done something which was wrong . . . certainly not anything punishable by death . . . but he evidently thought that God was punishing him. But once he made the realization that GOD LOVED HIM, he was no longer sick. The little fellow made use of that GREAT POWER—THE POWER TO CHOOSE. It gave him life. It saved the family much sorrow and heartache.

Too many people have the very bad habit of telling their children that God will punish them if they do something wrong. The child is filled with fear . . . the fear of God. He chooses to be afraid of God. The child goes into adult life . . . still with this fear. Is it any wonder that the average person's life is a shadow of what real living could be? He, in turn, does the same thing with his children. And so, century after century, this fear is perpetuated by parents who fail to understand that THE POWER TO CHOOSE can change their lives. If telling the child that God will punish him would

prevent the evil doing, it would be all right
. . . but look around and you will see that
it has not turned the trick. On the other
hand, if we would realize *that the wrong
doing itself carries with it its own punish-
ment,* then we will CHOOSE what is right.
Because we will then know that it isn't God
that is going to punish us, but it is our own
BAD CHOOSING that carries the punish-
ment with it. If we make the right choice in
the first place, what can go wrong?

For example, a woman who had a very
lovely son was constantly in the habit of
telling her little boy that if he did not do
what was right, God would punish him. The
result was that the little fellow was always
having colds. The mother was beside herself; she didn't know what to do. Then she
learned that you don't say that to a child.
You tell a child that God loves him. She explained this to the child, with the result that
the child no longer had any colds. The
mother was amazed and astounded. Here
you can see as long as the mother CHOSE
to tell her youngster that God would punish
him, he was filled with colds . . . when
she CHOSE to tell her son that GOD
LOVES YOU, the change came about.
WHAT   BROUGHT   ABOUT   THE
CHANGE? Did God make the change? It

was the mother, who in CHOOSING THE
RIGHT IDEA OF PRESENTING GOD
changed her child's life and her own.

We must, therefore, realize that there is
NOTHING OUTSIDE OF OURSELVES to
hurt us. GOD DOESN'T HURT US. GOD
LOVES US. THEREFORE, WHAT CAN
HURT US . . . *ONLY OUR OWN BAD
CHOOSING.*

If we choose to eat so much that we make
ourselves sick, who is to blame? If we
choose to drive our cars so fast that we cannot control them, who is to blame? If we
choose to allow ourselves to have nasty, disagreeable personalities, who is to blame? If
we try to become the "richest man in the
cemetery" and make ourselves invalids,
who is to blame? If we have failed to learn
how to live, whom shall we blame? God?
Oh, no! not any more. GOD LOVES YOU.
He doesn't hurt anybody. We hurt ourselves
through the bad use of this GREAT
POWER that God gave us . . . THE
POWER TO CHOOSE.

Choosing Wealth

-»»-»»-»»(((-(((-(((-

MILLIONS OF PEOPLE ARE SEEKING
wealth. They would like to be able to
say to themselves, "Now, I don't have to
worry about money anymore." They would
love to be free from money worries. So they
scheme, plan and try many different ways
to help themselves financially and nothing
seems to work. The result is that they become discouraged, and decide that they are
not the ones who will achieve this enviable
position. They tried everything but changing their thoughts—the one thing that would
make the difference.

Some time ago we came in contact with a
man who was having all kinds of financial
trouble. His wife complained that she was
afraid to go to the door, because the only
people who came to the door were bill col-
lectors. It was a very discouraging situation. We gave this family a book that we

thought would help them improve their thinking. The wife looked at the book and said, "I wouldn't read that stuff . . . there is nothing to it." The husband said, "I'll read it, leave it here." The result was that the man began to think differently. He showed a new spirit for living. Within a year's time, they moved into a better neighborhood; they bought a whole houseful of new furniture; he even made a down payment on a new car.

We did not give the man any money. Certainly money would have helped him, but it would only have been a temporary lift. What we did do was to start the man on the right road of CHOOSING HIS THOUGHTS FOR IMPROVING HIS FINANCIAL STATUS. That is what we need, if we are going to improve our financial positions. If we do not change our thinking, we can never hope to change our financial positions. What most of us fail to realize is that A TOOTH GROWS FROM THE INSIDE OUT. So, we must change our inner thoughts . . . as we change our inner thoughts about our financial positions, the outward change is bound to come about. So LET US CHOOSE GOOD, HEALTHY THOUGHTS ABOUT MONEY AND FINANCES.

By using this GREAT POWER TO

CHOOSE in the right direction, you are bound to improve your financial station. But too many people through their own failure to use this great power have made themselves slaves to the very thing they have wanted to avoid. There was a young man for whom life had been quite a struggle. He had been unemployed for quite a length of time. He finally obtained employment that was by no means anything to be proud of. Yet, this same young man, who was married and had a youngster, had the nerve to say, "I don't want to be rich." He was trying to set aside a few pennies every day so that his son would be able to go to college some day. This man was wise enough to choose to set aside a little money for his son's education. To say that it was a struggle is putting it mildly. He refused to go to a downtown movie, instead preferred to go to a neighborhood show, in order to save a quarter. He refused to go to a better type restaurant because it would cost more money. When he went to the legitimate theater, he would buy balcony seats, instead of orchestra, because that was all that he could afford. When he bought a car, he bought the most economical kind of car. He was unable to take his family on a vacation, because he couldn't afford

to do it. This man had the nerve to choose to
say, "I don't want to be rich."

Is it any wonder that millions of people
are steeped in poverty? NOT REALIZING
IT, THEY CHOOSE TO REMAIN POOR.
THEY FAIL TO RECOGNIZE THIS
GREAT POWER. No one can be blamed
for being economical. Many people must be
thrifty or they would not get along at all.
But these same people could be making use
of this GREAT POWER TO CHOOSE.
They could start to fill their minds with the
better things of life.

Instead, we hear day after day people
saying, "I would like that, but I can't afford
it." "I can't afford it." "I can't afford it."
It's true, BUT DON'T SAY IT. As long as
you continue to say "I CAN'T AFFORD
IT . . . *you will go all through your life*
with "I CAN'T AFFORD IT." CHOOSE A
BETTER THOUGHT. Say, "I'll buy it. I'll
get it." When you build up the thought that
you will get it, that you will buy it, you
build up the thought of expectancy. YOU
BUILD UP YOUR HOPE. NEVER DE-
STROY YOUR HOPE. When you destroy
your hope, then you have created for yourself a life of difficulty and disappointment.

A young man who didn't have a dollar to

his name said, "One of these days, I am going to Europe." A friend sitting by started
to laugh and said, "Look who's talking."
Twenty years later the man and his wife
went to Europe. This man did not say, "I
want to go to Europe and I suppose I never
will be able to afford it." He had the hope.
The hope gave him spirit. The spirit moved
him to do things so that he would be able to
go to Europe. When you say "I can't afford
it". . . everything stops. The hope is gone
. . . the mind becomes dulled . . . the
spirit is gone . . . then WE CHOOSE to
believe that nothing can be done about it.
THIS   GREAT   POWER . . . THE
POWER TO CHOOSE will give you the
necessary hope, the necessary spirit, the
necessary courage to carry on and GET
THE THINGS FROM LIFE THAT YOU
REALLY WANT.

Allen in his little book "As a Man Think-
eth" says that "Thoughts are Things." We
like to change it to read THOUGHTS BE-
COME THINGS. The telephone was a
thought in the mind of Bell before it became a telephone. The harvester was a
thought in the mind of McCormick before it
became a harvester. The electric bulb was a
thought in the mind of Edison before it became an electric bulb. John D. Rockefeller

when he didn't have a dime to his name
said, "Some day I am going to become a
millioniare." AND HE DID. So you must
realize that the things that you want out of
life are thoughts first before they become
things. Our financial condition is a thought
first, and then a reality. If we want to
change our financial picture, we must first
CHANGE OUR THOUGHT. If we
CHOOSE TO CHANGE OUR INNER
THOUGHTS . . . our outer conditions
must change. THAT'S THE LAW. When
you choose thoughts of "I can't afford it"
. . . I'll never get it . . ."I am one of the
blessed poor". . . you are blocking the
pathway to YOUR GOOD. CHOOSE
YOUR THOUGHTS . . . YOU CAN . . .
CHANGE YOUR THOUGHTS . . . YOU
CAN . . . use your imagination in the beginning, if necessary. You will never re-
gret it. Things will begin to happen for you,
changes will come into your life, such as
you never believed possible. YOU WILL
TRULY GAIN A NEW LEASE ON LIFE.

It is surprising how many times THIS
GREAT POWER . . . THE POWER TO
CHOOSE . . . if used correctly could
make a person's life what he wants it to be.
One young man had a very unusual experi-
ence. He found that every time he saved up

to seventy dollars, something would happen. He would have an accident . . . some unforeseen difficulty would arise . . . HE JUST COULDN'T SAVE OVER SEVENTY DOLLARS. This man will go through life with this problem and difficulty, unless he uses this GREAT POWER . . . THE POWER TO CHOOSE and starts to think differently.

Another man found that every time he had a little money in the bank . . . something would happen so that he JUST COULDN'T KEEP IT for any length of time. He went through his whole life with this thought . . . he could have just as easily used his GREAT POWER . . . THE POWER TO CHOOSE . . . and changed this thought destroyer.

One young man was a jack-of-all-trades. He was able to do many things well. Although he was successful in everything that he did, nevertheless, he never made any money. People could not understand why. He was ambitious. He was likable. He had a pleasing personality, but financially, he struggled year after year. Finally this young man had it pointed out to him just what his trouble was. He constantly made the statement, "I can do everything well but make money." Once he began to realize that his big trouble was simply a bad choice of thought . . . things began to change. Instead of saying, "I can do everything well but make money," he began to say, "I can do everything well, including making money." Within a few years' time this man's financial condition changed. He really and truly started to make money. He began to get ahead financially, until today, people say that he is a rich man. This man could have gone through his whole life doing many things well, but never making any money. As soon as he realized that he was CHOOSING THE WRONG THOUGHT, and did something about changing that thought, then his financial condition turned for the better. THE POWER TO CHOOSE brings about a much better and effective money-making power.

Choosing Conditions

>>>->>>->>><<<-<<<-<<<-

ANYONE WITH A LITTLE COMMON SENSE
knows that you cannot control conditions. Unless, of course, you happen to become the head of your government, and
maybe then you would be able to control
them.

But for most of us, we must agree that we
cannot control conditions. This is true. So,
what can we do? We can control our
thoughts . . . and by controlling our
thoughts . . . by USING THIS GREAT-
EST POWER . . . THE POWER TO
CHOOSE . . . we are INDIRECTLY
ABLE TO CONTROL CONDITIONS. The
most common illustration is in time of war.
A young man is called into the service. Here
he has no choice. He must go and serve his
country. He is brought to camp. Here he is
trained. He is prepared for action. All during this time HE HAD NO CHOICE as to
what his officers made him do. He had to

comply with their demands. BUT HE STILL HAD THE POWER TO CHOOSE HIS OWN THOUGHTS. If he chose the thought that he would not come out alive, that he would be crippled . . . it wouldn't be a surprise that this is exactly what happened. We know that on the other hand, that a person or soldier can protect himself through his own POWER TO CHOOSE. F. L. Rawson, noted engineer, and one of England's greatest scientists, in his book, "Life Understood," gives account of a British regiment under control of Colonel Whittlesey, which served in the World War for more than four years without losing a man. This unparalleled record was made possible by means of active cooperation of officers and men in memorizing and repeating regularly the words of the 91st Psalm which has been called the Psalm of Protection. This is an extreme case of the POWER TO CHOOSE, but remember it is the GREATEST POWER THAT MAN POSSESSES.

We all know that there are good times and bad times. Some people can't even make a living in good times, let alone in bad times, mainly because they have failed to use THIS GREATEST POWER . . . THE POWER TO CHOOSE. When bad times come along, most people sit back, fill themselves with discouragement and wait for the government to do something about it. Others will use this GREATEST POWER . . . THE POWER TO CHOOSE . . . and will make a success even in bad times. Many of our greatest businesses have been started and built in "so-called" bad times. Why? Because the founders of the business refused to believe in bad times . . . they went ahead anyway . . . and succeeded. In bad times, there are many times the number of advantages which good times do not allow. Less money is needed to start and keep the business going, help is easier to get and cheaper, competition is not so alert . . . and more than anything else, there are so many discouraged people that the PERSON WITH A LITTLE COURAGE doesn't have to battle so hard.

There was a man who was in business during one of the "bad time" periods. He felt that the reason he was not doing so well was due to the bad times. He felt that unless conditions improved, there would be no opportunity for him to improve. Then during the very heart of the bad time period, he went into a certain shopping district. He noticed that there were two butchers within ten stores of one another. One was as busy as he could be. People were standing three and four deep to be waited on. The other butcher hardly had a customer. Here is a problem. Bad times exist. Yet within the very same neighborhood there are two butchers, one who doesn't even know there is such a thing as bad times, and the other one is barely making a living. The young business man decided to investigate. He went into the store where the people were standing waiting for service, and as he did, the store owner said, "How do you do?" in a very pleasing and courteous manner, "I am busy, but I will be with you in a few minutes." He was gentle and kind with each and every customer. He was helpful and serviceable to people. He made suggestions to his customers, but at no time argued with them. The purchase was made. Then several days later, the young business man went to the other store. The proprietor growled, "What is it you want?" Instead of giving the young man the meat he wanted, this butcher attempted to force upon him, the meat the butcher thought he ought to have. He was not pleasant at all, and was interested only in his own immediate welfare. Here you can quickly recognize THE POWER TO CHOOSE.

The one butcher chose to believe that business was bad, due to the bad times, and that was the way it worked out for him. He was not a courteous and reasonable person with his customers. Furthermore, he even preferred to take his "bad business" out on the very people who came in to patronize him. The other butcher chose to believe that business was up to him. It was up to him to be fair and reasonable. It was up to him to be courteous and helpful. He didn't know what bad times were. He chose correctly. The man with little to do chose incorrectly. This ability TO RECOGNIZE THIS GREATEST POWER . . . THE POWER TO CHOOSE . . . makes it possible for a person to get the most out of life, while the other person not recognizing this power makes life a burden. THE POWER TO CHOOSE helps one to increase his money-making ability.

The young business man, after noticing the difference between the two butchers, went to his office the next day and started to work. HE CHOSE TO BELIEVE IT WAS UP TO HIM . . . not to the times or the government. He started to advertise, he made special sales, he made necessary changes for the times, he modified his prices, and before long he was busy again . . . business was good again . . . he was making money again. CONDITIONS HAD

NOT CHANGED. BUT HE DID. Through
this GREATEST POWER . . . THE
POWER TO CHOOSE . . . instead of
closing his doors, his business was once
more on its feet . . . he had changed . . .
even though the times had not.

In the field of employment, we have a
similar situation. Let us take two employees
and compare them and see how THE
POWER TO CHOOSE AFFECTS EACH
PERSON. One always chooses to be to work
on time. He chooses to follow instructions.
He chooses to do his work the very best that
he knows how. He chooses to offer suggestions which may help the business. He
chooses to do certain little odds and ends
which may not be in his keeping with the
position for which he was hired. He chooses
to work a few minutes, or even an hour overtime if necessary. He chooses to study the
business, even taking special courses after
working hours to improve himself and the
services of the company. This man, through
his simple POWER TO CHOOSE, makes
himself a successful employee who is bound
to make progress. He makes himself so
valuable to his employer, that his employer
goes out of his way, if necessary, to keep
this person employed.

Now let us take a look at the other kind

of employee. He chooses to come to work at a time suitable to himself. He chooses to argue with his employer and his fellow-workers, about certain things which have to be done. He refuses to work a few minutes or an hour overtime. He chooses to go outside of the business and talk against his company. He chooses to do only as much work as he is paid for. He chooses to spend his time in foolish entertainment and ungainly activities. He chooses to feel that the time outside of working hours belongs to him and he may do with it as he pleases. He chooses to refuse to look into the future, or to prepare himself for the future.

When bad times come around, the second man will be the first one let out. He will blame the times. He starts to complain bitterly because he lost his job. He will rant against his government, calling the heads of his government all kinds of nasty names. He will blame everybody but himself. His family and associates suffer along with him. He chooses to let the days and years go by. He finally finds himself in a home for the aged, which is kept up by the state. Why?

If there were only some way that people could be made to realize that THIS GREATEST POWER . . . THE POWER TO CHOOSE and choose correctly *EXISTS*

WITHIN THEIR OWN MINDS, that they
could carry out the plans of their own choice
and really live the way they may have
dreamed of living. It is easy enough to
blame conditions; it is easy enough to blame
relatives; it is easy enough to blame the government; it is easy enough to blame anybody and everybody and everything, if
ONE CHOOSES TO DO SO. But, any person who truly recognizes this GREATEST
POWER . . . THE   POWER   TO
CHOOSE . . . begins to make progress,
not only in his business life, but also in his
social, family and personal life. He begins
to realize that he is the one THAT IS DO-
ING THE CHOOSING and that friends, although they mean well, cannot do his choosing for him, nor can his relatives. Conse-
quently, he develops real self-confidence
based upon his own ability, upon his own
actions, and upon his own initiative. No
longer does he depend upon conditions. No
longer does he depend upon some figure of
imagination, but instead, he depends upon
himself; the results begin to tell right from
the beginning of his realization. *This realization seems so difficult because hundreds
of thoughts are racing through our minds at
such speed that we fail to recognize this
simple yet amazing POWER TO CHOOSE.*

Choosing Your Personality

>>>->>>->>> <<<-<<<-<<<

ONE OF THE GREATEST PROBLEMS IN life is the problem of personality. Personalities seem to be clashing constantly. Many of our troubles and difficulties come about because people cannot get along with one another. Homes are broken up, friendships are destroyed, employment problems by the hundreds arise because of a clash of personalities . . . and even wars are engaged in because of different nations failing to see eye to eye.

Here again the GREATEST POWER man possesses THE POWER TO CHOOSE plays a most important part. Stop to think about it . . . you can choose to be friendly or you can choose to be unfriendly. You can choose to be helpful, or you can choose to refuse to help. You can choose to be cooperative or you can choose to be stubborn. You can choose to get excited or you can choose to be calm. You can choose to lose your temper or you can choose to overlook the matter which would ordinarily cause you to be upset. You can choose to be lovable or you can choose to be bitter. You can choose to smile or you can choose to walk around with a long face. You can choose to be trusting or you can choose to distrust everyone you meet. You can choose to believe that "everybody is against you" or you can choose to believe that everybody likes you. You can choose to be neat and clean or you can choose to be careless and slovenly. You can choose to be lazy or you can choose to be ambitious. Stop to think about it AGAIN. Don't you do your own choosing? YOU CERTAINLY DO. Here is one of the best cases on record.

Benjamin Franklin came to the strange awakening that he was constantly losing friends. He began to realize that he was constantly arguing with people. HE JUST COULDN'T GET ALONG WITH PEOPLE. One day, around New Year's Day, when New Year's resolutions are generally made, he sat down and made a list of all his nasty personality characteristics. He listed them one by one. He arranged them, putting the most harmful trait at the top of the list, down to the least harmful. Then he decided that he would eliminate these nasty personality characteristics one by one. Each time that he found that he had successfully eliminated one, he would cross it off the list, until he had cleaned up the entire list. He developed one of the finest personalities in America. Everybody looked up to him and admired him. When the colonies needed help from France, they sent Franklin. The French liked Franklin so well that they gave him what he asked for. TODAY IN ALMOST ALL YOUR BOOKS ON PERSONALITY BUILDING, THE NAME OF BENJAMIN FRANKLIN is cited as the most outstanding case of personality development.

Suppose on the other hand, Franklin had CHOSEN to go through life without doing anything about his personality. Suppose Franklin had done what millions of people are doing today . . . using their personalities just as it was given to them by nature and their parents. Suppose that Franklin continued his argumentative ways . . . he never would have succeeded in getting the French to help the colonies, and the entire history of the United States would have been changed. ONE PERSONALITY made a great difference to a nation. And yet, mil-

lions of people are walking around and say-
ing, "What can I do about it?" How do you
know? How do you know what YOU might
be able to do as the years go by. Lincoln
said, "I will prepare myself and some day
my time will come." AND IT DID. HE
CHOSE TO BELIEVE in preparedness. AT
LEAST WE WILL MAKE LIFE REASON-
ABLE AND ENJOYABLE FOR THOSE
AROUND US. AT LEAST WE WILL NOT
BE RESPONSIBLE FOR BRINGING UN-
NECESSARY TROUBLE TO THOSE
ABOUT US.

How many times does one member of a
family make life miserable for everybody
else in the family? How often does an un-
reasonable father or maybe even a mother
make all the other members of the family
wish that they had never been born into that
family. One person can destroy or make an
entire family miserable. YET, THIS SAME
PERSON, BY USING THE GREATEST
POWER GIVEN TO MAN . . . THE
POWER TO CHOOSE . . . COULD
HAVE MADE A BEAUTIFUL LIFE FOR
THOSE AROUND HIM AND ESPE-
CIALLY THE MEMBERS OF HIS OWN
IMMEDIATE FAMILY. If each one of us
would make his own family life a pleasant

and enjoyable experience, THE WHOLE
WORLD COULD BE CHANGED IN A
VERY SHORT TIME.

One problem that faces many people as
they go through life is the loss of a beloved
one. So many people, after losing a mother,
father, brother, or a close friend or relative,
become so upset that life to them becomes
meaningless. "What is there to live for
now?" they ask. All over the world there
are thousands upon thousands of people
who walk through the streets and through
the balance of their lives "living corpses."
Failing to realize that they possess this
GREATEST POWER . . . THE POWER
TO CHOOSE . . . they continue their
lives choosing to be a burden to themselves
and everyone around them. You cannot
blame these people, for their loss was great.
The shock may have been very sudden, for
apparently no reason. They are unable to
analyze why it had to happen. Sometimes it
is not easy to analyze why it happened. But
whether we can analyze it or not, the important job on hand now is what to do with
the balance of life that remains to the one
left behind.

We feel that the best way to answer this
great question is through a story that we
came across some time ago. A young college

football star lost his mother the week before the "big game." The coach didn't know what to do. He had never had an experience like this before. He finally decided that he would leave it up to the young star himself. If the boy decided to play, that would be fine with the coach. However, if the young man decided that the shock was too great and that he would decide not to play, then the coach would abide by his decision. The day of the game came. The team ran out on the field. The young star was with them. The team proceeded to go through with their practice signals, while the young football star went over to the stands. He stood there. About twelve rows up in the stand there was an empty seat. It was draped in black. The young man stood there . . . looked at the empty seat draped in black and said, "Mother, I am playing this game for you." He then went into the game and helped his team to victory.

Here is a splendid illustration of the POWER TO CHOOSE. This young man could have sat down and started to cry. He could have made himself the subject of sympathy from all his fellow teammates. He could have made them all feel so sorry that the entire team would have been affected and the game would have been lost.

But he chose for the benefit of all. He benefited, his team benefited, and surely, his mother wherever she was, was really proud of her son. He was playing the WAY SHE WOULD HAVE WANTED HIM TO. That is the answer. After the beloved one has passed on, what can we do about it? Go on living THE WAY THEY WOULD WANT US TO LIVE. MAKE THEM PROUD OF US WHEREVER THEY ARE. True, we cannot control conditions . . . but we can control our power to choose. In controlling our POWER TO CHOOSE, we can make life interesting and worthwhile to ourselves and everyone else around us.

We look at all the problems of life and they seem insurmountable. We look around and we wonder, if life will ever be worthwhile. Some people will go so far as to say that the world is getting worse instead of better. The world will start getting better the very minute WE CHOOSE TO MAKE IT BETTER. Do not wait for the other fellow to start improving the world. Do not wait for your neighbor to start improving himself . . . YOU START. If each one of us will start to CHOOSE TO IMPROVE HIMSELF, WE CAN CHANGE OUR OWN LITTLE WORLDS, THE LITTLE WORLD THAT EACH AND EVERYONE OF US

LIVE IN. THAT'S THE MOST IMPOR-
TANT ONE FOR US. *THAT IS THE ONE
WE CAN DO SOMETHING ABOUT*. Each
one of us may have five or a hundred and
five people that we come in contact with. If
we have a pleasant and helpful influence on
these five or one hundred and five, our influence on them will be for the better . . .
they in turn will influence others in a similar manner . . . it won't take as long as
you might think to change this world to be a
BETTER PLACE TO LIVE IN.

Some time ago we saw an article in the
paper about a certain street that was to be
made into a boulevard by the governmental
authorities. The plans were all made and
everybody sat back and waited for the powers that be to start to make the necessary im-
provements. It was going to be a "million
dollar boulevard." But something happened. The government officials found it
impossible to go ahead with the plans and
the idea was tabled. One man who lived on
the boulevard CHOSE TO DO SOME-
THING ABOUT IT. He decided that if the
government officials were not going to beautify the boulevard, the least he could do
was to beautify his own front yard. This he
did. It was one of the most attractive places
on the boulevard. His neighbor saw what he

did and the neighbor began to beautify his place; this continued with each neighbor, until the entire boulevard looked like the "million dollar boulevard." WHO DID IT? Actually, ONE MAN. HE CHOSE TO START AND EVERYBODY ELSE FOL- LOWED. Don't say that you can't change the world. YOU CAN CHANGE YOUR LITTLE WORLD . . . and that's the one that counts. YOU CHOOSE TO THINK THAT YOU CAN CHANGE IT . . . THE NEXT FELLOW WILL GET THE IDEA AND IT WILL BE DONE . . . AND YOU CAN BE THE VERY PERSON TO START IT IN YOUR OWN HOME, JOB, COMMUNITY, OR EVEN IN YOUR COUNTRY.

Practically every personality problem could be solved if we would ONLY CHOOSE TO FOLLOW one simple little suggestion. So many husbands and wives are living miserable family lives because of various disagreements. Millions of people working on jobs are having their hands full because of many different forms of disa- greements. Even nations find themselves at war because of unsettled disagreements. If these people involved would use this GREATEST POWER GIVEN TO MAN . . . THE POWER TO CHOOSE . . . we would find ourselves in an altogether different style of living. Many, many years ago a wise old philosopher said,

"IF WE MUST DISAGREE . . . LET US DISAGREE WITHOUT BEING DISAGREEABLE."

If we would realize as individuals, if we would realize as husbands and wives, that two people living together are bound to have differences of opinion . . . that it is perfectly alright to disagree . . . BUT WITHOUT BEING DISAGREEABLE . . . THE ENTIRE NATIONAL PICTURE OF MARRIAGE WOULD CHANGE OVERNIGHT. Marriage could be so much more enjoyable. Home life could be so much more worthwhile. The influence on the children would be tremendous. The divorce rate would be cut so deeply, it would be unbelievable.

The great difference of opinion in the minds of employees is such that millions of people are unhappy in their work. Many times, these people find that they like the work, they like the pay, they enjoy the surroundings, but THEY CANNOT GET ALONG WITH CERTAIN PEOPLE. Thousands are constantly changing jobs, because of differences of opinions. If these people would use this GREATEST POWER

Your Greatest Power

. . . THE POWER TO CHOOSE . . .
and disagree without being disagreeable
. . . they would find themselves much happier, much more enjoyably engaged in their
work, and much freer and easier with the
people they come in contact with. It would
be a great burden off their shoulders, because instead of fighting people and conditions, they would be more alerted to un-
derstanding others and their opinions.

Most of us have had the experience of going through one or two wars or even more.
We have observed that it is one thing to win
a war and another thing to win the peace.
It is most interesting when you think about
it, that the very nation you defeat in war,
you must, after the war, feed and clothe,
help the conquered nation to its feet again,
give her financial aid so that her economy
will be self-sustaining. To what end? One
never knows. To start another conflict? To
recreate the very thing you sought to destroy? Will the nations of the world some
day use this GREATEST POWER . . .
THE POWER TO CHOOSE . . . and save
themselves these great catastrophies? Will
the nations of the world some day CHOOSE
TO DISAGREE WITHOUT BEING DIS-
AGREEABLE? Let us hope they will.
THEY CAN. Just as we can use this

GREATEST POWER . . . THE POWER
TO CHOOSE . . . to make our own individual lives worthwhile and enjoyable;
just as we can use this POWER TO
CHOOSE to make our family lives agreeable and happy, so can the nations of the
world make the family of nations, one
GREAT BIG HAPPY FAMILY. Sounds
too wonderful? WE HAVE THE POWER
. . . WE CAN, IF WE CHOOSE TO.

How can one be so sure? Go to a symphony sometime, or watch a great symphony
orchestra on the television. What do you
see? A hundred men or more playing one
great musical selection. Notice a little more
and you will see many, many different kinds
of instruments, each making its own sound
and contributing its own bit to the entire
musical selection. Different instruments,
yes . . . but disagreeing . . . not at all.
Each player plays for the good of all. No
conflicts . . . all in harmony. Each player
desires to make the selection the most bril-
liant piece of music ever played. Each man
gains pleasure in making this great production possible. Each man's pride swells as he
notices the great musical selection draw to
its close.

Analyze this great symphonic orchestra
a little closer and what do you find. Each

man chose to play in the orchestra. Each man chose to play the particular instrument that he was using. Each man chose to harmonize with the other players. Each man chose to do the best that he knew how. He chose to follow the conductor, as he directed them through the selection.

SO CAN WE. We have been given this power. We have been given this GREATEST POWER . . . THE POWER TO CHOOSE . . . by the GREAT CONDUCTOR. THE GREAT CONDUCTOR LOVES US. THE GREAT CONDUCTOR WANTS US TO GET ALONG. YES, WE ARE ALL DIFFERENT. Different customs, different foods, different mannerisms, different languages, but not so different that we cannot get along with each other . . . IF WE WILL DISAGREE WITHOUT BEING DISAGREEABLE. THE GREAT CONDUCTOR has often been referred to as OUR FATHER. Being OUR FATHER, he has made it possible to live together as one great peaceful family. He has made it possible, by giving US THE POWER TO CHOOSE. WILL WE USE IT SENSIBLY OR WILL WE USE IT FOOLISHLY? WE HAVE THE POWER . . . THIS GREATEST POWER . . . THE POWER TO CHOOSE.

Choosing Happiness

-»»-»»-»» «««-«-«-

ALMOST EVERYONE COULD FIND HIMSELF one hundred to five hundred per cent happier, if he could recognize and realize that he possesses THIS GREATEST POWER . . . THE POWER TO CHOOSE. . . . So many people have a little happiness and then try to hang on to it. Some people as soon as they find themselves a little happy, wonder what is wrong and especially begin to wonder if it will last. There was a play on Broadway in which the heroine walks out on the stage (she had just returned from her honeymoon) and states she is so happy "she could die." Just imagine . . . here is a person who was searching for happiness . . . now that she has it "she could die." What a terrible MISUSE of the GREATEST POWER . . . THE POWER TO CHOOSE? Is it any wonder that we see so little happiness? Those who have it are so afraid that they cannot hold on to it, that they lose it almost as fast as they find it.

Sometime ago a young man told us this story. He said, "I was going with a young lady. We became very fond of each other. We decided to become engaged. So happy were we in our engagement that we decided to culminate our happiness in marriage. We were married. We fixed up a very attractive little apartment. In fact, it was the envy of all our friends. My wife was working. I was working. We had a car. We had a little money in the bank. We were really and truly living a heaven on earth. But, from time to time, I would talk with some of my friends, and they seemed to feel that it wouldn't last. They told me that it couldn't last. They would say, 'Look at the Joneses, how happy they were the first few months of their married life. Look at them now, how much trouble and worry they have. Look at the Smiths. They were happy, too, the first few months of their married life. Look how unhappy they are now.' I heard this so many times that I thought that my wife and I were living an unnatural life instead of a natural one, that any day this heaven-on-earth marriage balloon would burst. I would go home, after talking to one of these people who said it was too good to last, and say the same thing to my wife. 'Dear, this is too good to last. It is too heavenly. It just can't go on.' Before long, things began to happen. My wife lost her job. I lost my job. We had to give up our car. We had to give up our beautiful little apartment that we had fixed up. We had to go back and live with mother, and on top of it all, my wife became a mother herself."

"What's the good of living," he cried out, "if every time you get things straightened out, something comes along to spoil it." He wanted to commit suicide. He felt that if THIS IS LIFE, then you might as well end it now.

We finally showed the young man that had he used his GREATEST POWER . . . THE POWER TO CHOOSE . . . HE COULD HAVE AVOIDED ALL OF THIS DIFFICULTY. We showed him that he did not have to CHOOSE TO BELIEVE his friends who told him that married happiness does not and cannot last. We told him about a wonderful statement that a woman wrote in her book that would have saved him all this difficulty. Florence Scovell Shinn, author of the "Game of Life and How to Play It" and also, "Your Word Is Your Wand" states in the latter book that *NOTH-*

ING IS TOO GOOD TO LAST. We explained to him that there isn't anything that
will come along to spoil your life, if you
use your POWER TO CHOOSE COR-
RECTLY. If you use your POWER TO
CHOOSE that NOTHING IS TOO GOOD
TO LAST, it is surprising but true, that
things will run along smoothly and beautifully for you, even beyond your fondest
dreams. *HERE IS THE SECRET OF
KEEPING THINGS RUNNING SMOOTH-
LY*. But, you must constantly remind yourself that when everything is going without
trouble that THAT IS THE WAY IT IS
SUPPOSED TO BE. The stars don't bump
into the moon; the moon does not crash into
the sun; the sun does not crash into the
earth. Certainly, if the stars and the moon
and the earth, traveling at a tremendous
pace don't conflict with one another, why
can't our lives run along smoothly without
the conflicting forces that so many people
encounter. Our lives can run along without
friction, if we could only realize the full
import of the POWER TO CHOOSE. THE
POWER TO CHOOSE THAT NOTHING
IS TOO GOOD TO LAST will make a
change in your life far greater than one
could even dream of. As one man said,
"Our heaven on earth is right here, but the

trouble with most of us is that we don't take advantage of it."

Everywhere you go you hear of people who are getting along beautifully, and then seem to have trouble holding on to this smooth living. A man is getting along exceptionally well in his work. He is happily married. He has money in the bank. He drives a big car. He is sitting on "top of the world." But can he stand it? No! He doesn't see anyone else living so smoothly. He thinks he is better than the next fellow. He becomes overconfident. Overconfidence always leads to carelessness. This carelessness leads him into trouble of one form or another. NOW HE IS DISCOURAGED. Didn't he have everything he wanted? Wasn't he happy? Didn't he go to church and live according to the rules? So he started to look for something to blame. He comes to the conclusion that there was something outside himself that caused his trouble. He didn't do anything to cause it. Certainly not. But let's analyze his case, and what do we find. He was getting along fine. He wasn't short in anything. He made one little mistake. He allowed himself to become overconfident. Instead of thanking God for his good fortune and choosing to keep it that way, he chose to become careless and . . .

not realizing, deliberately choosing to do something to GET BACK INTO TROUBLE AGAIN. This overconfidence has done as much to spoil and frequently to ruin as many lives as any other reason we might know of. Very little is ever said about overconfidence. We are not aware of it. It overtakes us because we have failed to recognize this GREATEST POWER . . . THE POWER TO CHOOSE . . . with the result that we are not careful at a time when we should be. Nature does not want us underconfident . . . but she does not want us to be overconfident. Millions of people have had a taste of overconfidence . . . without recognizing it. If they don't recognize it, they may be kicked down by it, and may never get up again. Then when it happens, it takes the spirit out of their lives. They are defeated and beaten. They cannot analyze what happened, with the result that another life joins the great ranks of discouraged people.

George gets a raise in salary. He comes home as happy as can be. He says to his wife, "Let's go out and celebrate." They call up another couple and go to some night club to celebrate. They start to drink. Before long George is making love to the other man's wife. His wife is now making love to the husband of the other couple. Now George doesn't like it. They start to argue. They come home in a rage. The argument continues into the early hours of the morning. After it is all over, George wishes he had never gotten the raise. Then, he sits down and begins to complain. He complains that his happiness did not last long, that his good luck was short-lived. But why? Because something outside himself brought it about? Because God did not want him to be happy? Why? You know why . . . now. George's good fortune made him overconfident. His overconfidence led to carelessness . . . carelessness almost always leads to trouble.

Most people cannot stand life when it runs along "TOO SMOOTHLY." They crave excitement. They crave it because they choose it. This choice brings them into a troubled state and then they say "THIS IS LIFE." Life did not produce the trouble. We bring it about ourselves with our BAD CHOICE OF THOUGHT.

From time to time we hear people say, "If I can put this deal across, then I don't care what happens." "If I marry George, then I don't care what happens." "After we get the mortgage paid, then I don't care what happens." WHAT A TERRIBLE

CHOICE OF THOUGHT! How stupid! Can you see why there is so much trouble in the world, and why so few people are really happy? Imagine choosing the thought . . . "I don't care what happens." It is almost like going into a restaurant and saying, "I don't care what you serve me as long as it is food." They may serve you food that is so badly burned that you can't even eat it. They may serve you meat that you can't even cut. They may serve a vegetable that is so badly rotted that you can't even look at it. BE CAREFUL. It is just as easy to be careful, as it is to be careless. YOU DO CARE WHAT HAPPENS AND YOU KNOW IT. Keep thinking good thoughts. Keep thoughts that will help you, not harm you. It is important, because through this GREATEST POWER . . . THE POWER TO CHOOSE . . . LIFE BECOMES WHAT YOU THINK AND CHOOSE IT TO BE.

Our parents, our grandparents, our great-grandparents and people for generations back have so completely filled our minds with the thought that we must have trouble; that this, that, and the other is too good to last; that we of this modern day and age have come to inherit these thoughts which *keep the world in mental bondage.*

Choosing Happiness

THE POWER TO CHOOSE gave the young man in our story a NEW FREEDOM. He slept better. He felt better. He realized that there was nothing outside himself trying to hurt him or destroy his happiness. He began to live. HE FOUND A NEW LEASE ON LIFE. He began to realize that there *WASN'T SOMETHING* THAT ALWAYS HAPPENS TO SPOIL HIS LIFE. *THAT SOMETHING* was his own failure TO CHOOSE CORRECTLY. Once he realized this simple, yet POWERFUL FORCE, his whole life changed. He knew that IT WAS HIS OWN THOUGHTS . . . HIS OWN CHOOSING that caused his trouble and not some unseen force or power outside himself. (Read this last statement again and again.)

All over the world people CHOOSE TO BELIEVE that if it isn't one thing, it's another. People everywhere are bewildered by the thought . . . if it isn't one thing, it's another. A man is working steadily . . . everything is moving along without friction . . . EVERYTHING EXCEPT HIS OWN THINKING. He starts his mind into action. He says, "Yes, I am working now, but how long will it last?" Before long, he is out of work. The grocery bill begins to mount; the back rent becomes a worry; work is not in

sight; his child takes sick; then he takes
sick. A big doctor bill faces him, together
with all the other expenses of the household.
The man has to go to the hospital. The hospital bill makes life even more uncomforta-
ble. Finally, the man goes back to work. He
begins to pay up his debts. He is just about
straightened out and paid up on all his bills
when something else appears . . . and so
. . . with a few experiences of this kind he
becomes a CONFIRMED BELIEVER in the
thought . . . THAT IF IT ISN'T ONE
THING, IT'S ANOTHER.

During all this trouble period, he found
himself carried away with his trouble and
his trouble thoughts. He never did think
clearly, mainly because he was never taught
to think clearly, and he just never did learn
to think clearly on his own. He had his
"ACRES OF DIAMONDS," but he never
found them. He remained poor in his
thoughts, and poor thoughts bring poor results. Had he discovered his GREAT-
EST POWER . . . THE POWER TO
CHOOSE . . . he would then have realized that most of his trouble was due to his
own poor thinking. THEN IF HE HAD
DISCOVERED THAT NOTHING IS TOO
GOOD TO LAST, he could have avoided his
difficulties and instead of expecting trouble,

he would have expected his smooth-running life to continue.

It isn't easy to live an even-going life, when we notice that everyone around us is filled with trouble, difficulties and disappointments. However, when we begin to realize that those who are filled with troubles and difficulties are using their GREAT. EST POWER . . . THE POWER TO CHOOSE . . . AND USING IT INCOR- RECTLY, then we begin to understand why things happen the way they do. Is it any wonder that so many people "knock on wood" when things are going along nicely. The fear THAT IT IS TOO GOOD TO LAST is obvious and apparent. We must constantly remind ourselves . . . THAT NOTHING IS TOO GOOD TO LAST . . . and before long we will begin to believe it. When enough of us begin to believe it and practice it . . . we will . . . just as Columbus discovered a new world in 1492 . . . DISCOVER A NEW WORLD OF REAL LIVING.

One of the greatest of religious leaders, head of one of the large Eastern religions, said, "How can I be happy, when the rest of the world is unhappy?" A very good question, and being a very wise man he presented a very interesting problem. How-

ever, if we see no man happy then we come
to the conclusion that life is not meant to
be happy. When we are happy for a short
time, we must of necessity come to the conclusion that it is not meant to last. But, why
not? If this great religious leader had said
instead, "Look at me . . . look how happy
I am . . . you can be the same as I . . .
if you will follow my teachings." Then his
millions of followers would have felt that it
is natural to be happy, and at least one of
the great religions of the world would have
had millions of happy people. Again, we
see that one man can change an entire group
of people, running into the millions. Like
many of our new inventions, no one thought
of them before. Likewise, before Florence
Shinn came out with the statement NOTH-
ING IS TOO GOOD TO LAST . . . people thought that happiness could not last
. . . because so few people had been able
to demonstrate it. This great religious
leader has THE POWER TO CHOOSE. He
chose to believe that he could not be happy
because the rest of the world was not. What
was to stop him from choosing to set an
example of happiness for his followers?
Nothing, but his OWN CHOICE.

The same conditions that prevail with an
individual can also prevail with a whole

country. So many people remember when everything in the nation was going along smoothly. Almost everybody was working, there was very little unemployment. People were buying new cars; stocks were high; property was high; everybody seemed to be making money. Most people seemed to be riding on the crest of the waves. For a short period of time it seemed as though the world was having one of the greatest periods of prosperity that it had ever seen. But many people from the richest to the poorest, from the weakest to the strongest, from the lowest to the highest walks of life, began to feel that IT WAS TOO GOOD TO LAST. Little by little this thought began to fill the minds of the people everywhere. Things began to change. People became cautious. Stocks began to topple. Banks began to close. Everywhere there was nothing but darkness and despair. A land that yesterday was prosperous, was now thrown into the depths of depression, all because from the richest to the poorest, people felt that IT WAS TOO GOOD TO LAST.

What would have happened if these same millions of people who said it was too good to last would have used their GREATEST POWER and had CHOSE TO BELIEVE THAT NOTHING IS TOO GOOD TO

LAST? THEY WOULD HAVE FOUND A WAY TO KEEP THINGS RUNNING ALONG SMOOTHLY. As one man said, "This is truly a great country." When the country seemed to be at a standstill and was not going forward, the automobile came along and kept everybody busy and progressive. When we seemed to catch up with ourselves with the automobile and it seemed that everything would be at a standstill, the airplane began to pick up the slack in our production. Then when the airplane seemed to fill its need, then radio began to take up the slack . . . after radio came television. THIS ONE MAN CHOSE TO BELIEVE THAT NOTHING IS TOO GOOD TO LAST. *SOMETHING GOOD CAN HAPPEN* . . . just as easily as something bad. WE MUST USE THIS POWER TO CHOOSE CORRECTLY OR IT WILL WORK THE VERY OPPOSITE OF THE WAY WE WOULD LIKE LIFE TO BE.

There are still millions upon millions of people in this world who have nothing. There are still millions upon millions of people on this earth who do not have a single change of clothing. Millions are not properly housed. The world as a whole is still unlearned and uneducated. According to the reports, two-thirds of the world still eat without knives and forks. Even in this country, there are still millions of people without bathtubs, without decent living quarters, without hope of ever seeing a better way of life.

LET US CHOOSE TO BELIEVE
THAT SOMETHING GOOD CAN
HAPPEN
WHY MUST WE ALWAYS USE
THE OLD MODEL . . . THAT
SOMETHING BAD WILL HAPPEN?

We begin to realize now that through the GREATEST POWER . . . THE POWER TO CHOOSE . . . that man has come a long way since the first man walked the face of the earth. The world, as a result of modern inventions is reaching a point that it is gradually mastering the forces of nature, in as far as the mechanical perfections that go to make life more enjoyable are endless. With this mastering of nature, we begin to realize now that we have a bigger job . . . MASTERING OURSELVES. We have gone through the stone age, the wood age, the iron age, just going through the mechanical age . . . we are now entering the MENTAL AGE. Man has been using . . . those who have used it . . . THE POWER TO

CHOOSE and not realizing it. Now that we realize it . . . we make the great discovery that most of our troubles, our difficulties, and our miseries are *MAN MADE*.

Man has been making himself a mechanical life of ease and pleasure; while at the same time he has been making his mental life more and more complicated. It need not be; not any more. NOW THAT HE HAS DISCOVERED THIS GREATEST POWER . . . THE POWER TO CHOOSE . . . HE CAN CHOOSE TO LIVE . . . LIKE A MAN.

No longer can man blame something outside of himself. Man must blame himself. Man does what he does because . . . HE CHOOSES THUS TO DO. Maybe we won't admit it, but it is true. For years man worked the whole day through, sometimes putting in twelve to fourteen hours a day, with little or no time for leisure. As a result of modern inventions, man has more time for himself. Man, therefore, is at the present time, beginning to fathom the art of real living. He must learn how to live because he has so much leisure time on his hands. As long as he has so much time on his hands, he must be able to use it sensibly. If he doesn't, he will bring destruction upon himself. Man has found that tasks that were difficult years ago, are now simplified by machinery. Man will now find time to learn how to live. In learning how to live, he will recognize that the most important task is TO LEARN HOW TO LIVE WITH HIM-SELF. He will learn to live with himself when he begins to use THE GREATEST POWER THAT HE POSSESSES . . . THE POWER TO CHOOSE.

This GREATEST POWER . . . THE POWER TO CHOOSE . . . will make life for him what he always wanted it to be; not to depend upon something outside of himself, but to depend on that great POWER WITHIN HIMSELF, THIS GOD-GIVEN POWER WHICH MAKES HIM A MAN. He will realize that life does not depend on money, machines, cars, homes, furs, and so-called wealth . . . but upon his MIND POWER given to him by the UNIVERSAL MIND POWER of which he is a part, and through which all that he desires can come to pass.

Man must realize that the most important thing in life is LIFE. Therefore, he owes his first duty to this LIFE which he possesses. If he takes care of his LIFE, it will be what he wants it to be. If he neglects his own LIFE . . . it will be what he does not want it to be. After the UNIVERSAL POWER

gives man LIFE . . . then it is up to MAN
TO CHOOSE TO DO WITH IT AS HE
SEES FIT.

May we remind you of a poem we came
across some time ago:

> *"I shall pass through this world but*
>   *once*
> *Any good, therefore, that I can do,*
> *Or any kindness that I can show*
> *To any human being,*
> *Let me do it now. Let me*
> *Not defer it or neglect it,*
> *For I shall not pass this way again."*

Therefore, the fact remains that inas-
much as we are going through life JUST
ONCE, we should choose to make life a
confident one, instead of a timid one . . .
that we should choose to make a calm life
rather than one of restlessness . . . that
we should choose to have poise rather than
confusion . . . that we should choose to
make the most of life for ourselves and
everyone else around us . . . rather than
spoil our own lives and those about us. We
have the POWER TO CHOOSE . . . LET
US USE IT TO THE BEST OF OUR
ABILITY. As we use our own minds to
CHOOSE THE BEST so we will find that

the UNIVERSAL MIND will come to our aid and assistance to help us choose the BEST. Together we cannot fail. WE MUST SUCCEED!

JUST AN AFTERTHOUGHT.

Now that you have read "YOUR GREATEST POWER," do you feel better? Sure you do. Then read it over and over again.

Anytime you find yourself a little disgusted, disturbed, or upset, read it. You'll feel better.

Keep a copy at your bedside. Read a little before you go to sleep. You will feel better and stronger the next morning.

*   *   *

Why not send a copy to someone who needs it? It will be appreciated, to be sure.